The Story
of the
Fourth Canadian Division
1916-1919

The Naval & Military Press Ltd

Published by

The Naval & Military Press Ltd
Unit 5 Riverside, Brambleside
Bellbrook Industrial Estate
Uckfield, East Sussex
TN22 1QQ England

Tel: +44 (0)1825 749494

www.naval-military-press.com
www.nmarchive.com

*In reprinting in facsimile from the original, any imperfections are inevitably reproduced
and the quality may fall short of modern type and cartographic standards.*

FOREWORD

In arranging for the publication of this little book, my object has been to give a concise picture of the general situation and intention at various stages in the career of the Division, in the hope that it may serve as a background on which each one can fix his individual part in the great performance.

Just as a performance on the stage is dependent in the end on the performances of the individuals, so the accomplishments of the Division have been made possible by the performances of Brigades, Battalions, Batteries, Platoons, and finally of individual soldiers, to whom all honour is due.

Detail has been sacrificed to brevity in order to get the volume into the hands of the members of the Division before embarking for Canada. It is not intended in any way as an official history, as such a publication, in much greater detail, is now in hand.

To the Officers, Non-Commissioned Officers and Men of the Division this little volume, compiled by Major C. B. Lindsey, D.S.O., of my General Staff, is dedicated.

D. Watson

MAJOR-GENERAL.

CONTENTS

	PAGE
FOREWORD	iii
STORY OF THE 4TH CANADIAN DIVISION ...	5
BATTLE ORDER (1/8/16)	24
BATTLE ORDER (1/8/17)	29
BATTLE ORDER (1/8/18)	35
BATTLE ORDER (8/3/19)	41
DATES OF INTEREST	47
MY FAREWELL ...	50

STORY OF THE 4th CANADIAN DIVISION

IN the spring of 1916 it was decided that another Canadian Division should be formed and take the field as soon as possible.

Accordingly, the 4th Canadian Division was organized at Bramshott Camp, Hants, under the command of Major-General Sir David Watson, K.C.B., C.M.G., and first came into being officially in May, 1916.

For four months all ranks devoted their attention to intensive training and to familiarizing themselves with the ever-changing appliances for warfare which were in use " out there." Many delays occurred during this period of training, the principal one being in June, when 8,000 picked men were sent from the Division as reinforcements to the Corps in France, by reason of the severe fighting and consequent casualties. It was recognized, however, that the interests of the Canadian Corps were paramount, and this spirit characterized the Division in this and all subsequent actions and operations.

Eventually, on the 10th August, 1916, the long-sought date arrived, and the Division commenced its move to France. (The Battle Order of the Division as it arrived in the Western Theatre is shown on page 24). Disembarking and entraining at Havre, the Hoograaf area was reached about August 14th.

The Battle of the Somme had commenced on the 1st July, and the turn of the Canadian Corps to do its share had arrived. The 1st, 2nd, and 3rd Divisions were to move at once, and were just waiting for relief. Accordingly the 4th Canadian Division relieved the 2nd Canadian Division and a portion of the 19th British Division in the Ypres-Comines Canal—Messines front, on the southern flank of the famous Ypres Salient, and came under the orders of the IX Corps. A few days were spent in "Schooling," and the Division commenced its maiden tour on August 25th, holding a frontage of over 8,000 yards.

For four weeks the seasoning process progressed. Successful raids were undertaken by all three Brigades, and whenever training facilities were available full advantage was taken to practise the fighting troops in the hints which were continually arriving from the Somme. The all-important Supply and Medical Departments "hit their stride," and the various parts of the whole machine were running smoothly and with confidence when, on October 23rd, the Division was relieved by the 4th Australian and 16th British Divisions, and started for the Somme. About one week was spent in the Second Army Training area at Tilques.

On October 11th the Division took over the Pys-Miraumont sector from the 3rd Canadian Division, coming under the orders of the II Corps, and prepared for the attack on Regina Trench, which took place on the 21st after several postponements. Owing to the bad weather, observation was extremely difficult, with the result that, on the right, the wire was not cut and the trench was not completely taken. Bad weather conditions continued, but on November 11th the line was carried well beyond Regina Trench.

On November 18th the Division attacked Desire and Desire Support Trenches with complete success, except on the right, where very heavy machine-gun fire held up the advance. Our arrangements to clean up this pocket were countermanded by higher authority, and accordingly the line as held was consolidated and handed over to the 51st British Division on November 28th.

For those who were there the appalling conditions of rain and mud under which these operations were carried out are more pleasant to forget. For the uninitiated any attempt at description is futile. It is sufficient to say that the spirit which carried men through this ordeal was the same spirit which has inspired the most gallant accomplishments in the records of the Canadian Corps.

On December 4th the Division rejoined the Canadian Corps in the Bruay-Divion Area, and, after a short rest, on December 21st took over a sector of the line south of the Souchez River on the steep slopes of the Vimy Ridge, relieving the 1st Canadian Division. The refitting of the Division was undertaken, and the periodical rests of the Reserve Brigade at Château de la Haie served to get the machine thoroughly re-organized. The fighting attention throughout the winter 1916-1917 was devoted to raiding and " strafing " the Hun. Also an enormous amount of work was done in preparation for the Battle of Vimy Ridge, notably the construction of Blue Bull, Vincent, Tottenham, and Cavalier Tunnels, some 12,000 linear feet in all.

On April 9th the Battle of Arras commenced, and with it the storming of the Vimy Ridge. On the first day a certain portion of Hill 145 held out against us by virtue of its very commanding position and the extremely stubborn resistance of large groups of the enemy. However, the situation was completely cleared up that night, and the next afternoon the line was pushed farther out on the eastern slopes of the ridge. On the day following our line was extended some 1,500 yards to the left, and the Division again attacked, this time capturing the commanding knoll known as the " Pimple." Again, on the 13th, the line was carried forward—this time to the line La Chaudiere-Bois de Givenchy, both inclusive—and by this time the Vimy Ridge was entirely in the hands of the Canadians.

The German resistance again stiffened, and as our communications had become considerably strung out over very difficult crater-torn ground, saturated with water, it was necessary to call a halt and construct proper roads before further determined offensive action could be taken. The difficulty of ammunition supply to the guns was extreme.

This halt afforded the enemy sufficient respite to collect himself and consolidate and strengthen his new line, so that by the time we were again in a position to resume the offensive the enemy was also thoroughly prepared for defence.

There followed a number of large raids and minor operations, resulting in the capture of La Coulotte, the Electric Generating Station, and the Railway Triangle. The fighting in these operations was particularly bitter, and their success was due very largely to the individual bravery and initiative of the troops.

On July 2nd the Division was withdrawn to Villers au Bois area to Corps Reserve, where training and refitting took place. The weather was fine, and sports were much in evidence.

To take Hill 70 was the next task set the Canadian Corps. The actual assault was to be made by the 1st and 2nd Canadian Divisions, but the 4th Canadian Division had an extremely important part as well. This was to work forward the line in front of Lievin, so that Lens might be attacked from a favourable position if opportunity offered, and also to create a diversion on this front, in the hope that the enemy might think the attack to be on a much larger scale than was the case. Both these tasks were successfully carried out. The line was taken forward over 1,000 yards right up to the well-known Green Crassier and Aconite Trench in face of severe resistance.

About the end of August the situation quietened down on this front, and normal reliefs were going on when the Division was suddenly ordered to Ypres along with the rest of the Canadian Corps.

The events which led up to the situation as we found it east of Ypres were as follows. The Allies had undertaken a major operation in July, with a view to freeing the Belgian Coast, and thus dislodging the bases from which the German submarines were operating in the Channel. For the first three weeks this attack had gone well, but from then on the German defence had been very well conducted. The country was generally adapted to defence, and the numerous " pill-boxes " which the enemy had built and the bad weather combined to make offensive operations extremely difficult. Most of the British Divisions on the western front had taken part in this offensive, and had been withdrawn exhausted, with the net result that our line had been advanced only as far as the foot of the Passchendaele Ridge. The enemy was thus enjoying good observation of our communications almost as far back as Ypres, and to allow him to retain this superiority throughout the forthcoming winter would be unwise, and it was therefore decided that the Hun must be pushed off the Ridge. The Canadian Corps was taken north to do the job.

The 4th Canadian Division took over from the 3rd Australian Division, and, with another Australian Division on its right and the 3rd Canadian Division on its left, attacked on October 26th and 30th. The allotted task was accomplished, and the line was carried forward beyond Crest Farm to the most favourable position available for the jump-off of the 2nd Canadian Division to the capture of Passchendaele Village and the beating of the Bosche from his position of observation. In fact, a number of our men were actually in Passchendaele, but were withdrawn to form up on the previously determined jumping-off line.

The condition of the weather and ground throughout this tour was very bad. The situation also was bad in two other respects. There was only one road for all traffic east of Ypres in our Army, and this road was continually subjected to gruelling enfilade artillery fire. Ypres was a " bottle-neck " through which all traffic in that part of Belgium had to pass, and around which many thousands of troops were bivouacked, and the German bombing planes came over at such frequent intervals throughout the day and night that rest was almost out of the question.

After Passchendaele the Corps again moved south

and took over its old front near the Vimy Ridge. The 4th Canadian Division remained a month in the Bruay-Auchel area, where the time was spent in training and refitting. Just before Christmas the Mericourt-Avion sector was taken over.

During this tour extensive raids were carried out, and an increase in the activity of the Bosche became noticeable.

Towards the end of February, 1918, the Division was again relieved, and moved to the Bruay-Auchel area, where further headway was made with training and the proper assimilation of the large drafts which had already come to replace the Passchendaele losses.

About the middle of March the Division returned to the line, and took over the Lens and St. Emile Fronts. Here the raiding, shelling, and gassing activities on both sides increased beyond anything experienced up to that time.

Since the disappearance of the Russian Front there had been ever-increasing signs that the enemy intended to make a big effort to smash the Allied Armies on the Western Front. Accordingly plans for certain changes in organization were made within the Canadian Corps, which were calculated to strengthen our fighting ability. These included in this Division the formation of a Brigade of Engineers, a third Machine Gun Company, and an increase in establishment of 100 other ranks per infantry battalion.

A policy of defence in great depth was adopted, and the various features of value to us were organized so as to afford facilities for defence either mutually or independently. Great attention was given to the machine-gun defence of the areas, and a large number of Champagne type emplacements were constructed.

The work accomplished on defences by the Division during the period in 1918 when the Allied Armies were on the defensive was very gratifying, and was in no small measure due to the feeling that the Vimy Ridge, which was so essentially Canadian, had been placed in our care.

On March 21st the long-expected German attack broke forth on the fronts of the Fifth and Third Armies, and it was soon apparent that the enemy was meeting with very considerable success. There was no evidence whatever of any depression within the Division as a result of these German successes.

The Canadian Corps was ordered to make further troops available to support the Third Army, with the result that the 4th Canadian Division was ordered to put its Third Brigade in line in the Hill 70 Section. It relieved the 1st Canadian Division on March 23rd-24th.

The Division was to be relieved on the 27th-28th by the 46th British Division, and pass into G.H.Q. Reserve in the Barlin area ; but on the morning of the 28th came a renewed enemy attack, this time extending north of the Scarpe, where the 56th British Division had been pressed back to the second line as far north as Gavrelle. All information from prisoners pointed to a renewal of the attack with fresh troops on the 29th against the southern end of the Vimy Ridge, and the situation was decidedly serious. By the morning of the 28th there were five reserve and support battalions of this Division in various stages of relief distributed between the line Fosse 11-Souchez and Barlin. These five battalions were placed under the orders of Brigadier-General V. W. Odlum, and designated as " Odlum's Special Brigade." By dawn on the 29th this Brigade concentrated near Mont St. Eloi, whence they were to move in support of the 56th Division in case of further attack. This sudden change of orders entailed great hardship for the troops concerned.

The expected attack did not come off, but the 4th Canadian Division was ordered to relieve the 56th Division by 29th-30th. The battalions of Odlum's Special Brigade returned to the orders of their own Brigadiers, and took over the line on 29th-30th. They came under orders of the 3rd Canadian Division until the 30th, when the remainder of the Division arrived and assumed command of the line in the Gavrelle-Oppy sector.

The line to which the British Divisions had withdrawn was originally intended as an intermediate support line, and was badly suited for a front line. Accordingly, another intensive period of defence construction was undertaken in which excellent progress was made. Transport line and all other available back-line personnel were grouped into platoons and told off to garrison certain localities echeloned in depth. Along with this work the necessity for prisoners and information was as pressing as ever, and so the raiding activity was kept up. However, no further attacks developed on this front.

April 9th saw the commencement of the big German drive in the north between La Bassee and Armentieres. Here again the enemy met with success, and in order to help supply reserves the Canadian Corps had to lengthen out its line until it was holding one-fifth of the length of the whole British line. Behind our lines we sent our Divisional Wing to form part of the two special brigades of infantry, and tunnellers which the Corps had organized ; we got more machine guns and some tanks to help in the defence, while in front of our line we did more raiding and made a greater display than ever. The bluff worked, for the Bosche never attempted any operation against our front, and, indeed, he showed distinct signs of nervousness at the activity we were displaying on the flank of his salient on the Lys.

In April the Division side-slipped north to include the Mericourt sector, where it continued to work and raid until May 7th, when it was relieved by the 51st Highland Division and the 52nd Lowland Division recently arrived from Palestine.

The Division, with the rest of the Corps (less the 2nd Canadian Division) then went out for the " long rest " in the Monchy Breton area, and went into G.H.Q. Reserve. One Brigade and one Machine Gun Company remained at Château de la Haie in support of the XVIII Corps in case of necessity. Several parties reconnoitred the Lys battle front with a view to operating either defensively or offensively in that area.

Most of the time was spent in training, for which the facilities were, on the whole, very good. The training was confined to open warfare, and many schemes involving the employment of tanks, artillery, trench mortars, engineers, machine guns, and aeroplanes in combination with infantry were carried out. Later attention was concentrated on platoon manœuvres, particularly with a view to overcoming machine-gun defence in depth. Extensive use was made of smoke grenades in these practices. The operations which ensuêd proved the soundness of this training.

On July 1st the usual Dominion Day celebrations were held. This year there were better opportunities than ever before, and full advantage had been taken of them. The natural amphitheatre at Tincques, together with the grand stand built of bridging material by the Engineers, and decorated as it all was, afforded at the same time an excellent and picturesque view of the stadium for the many thousands of troops who attended. The long period in reserve had afforded ample opportunity for thorough training and satisfactory eliminations, with the result that all the events were well contested and times were good. Altogether this was one of the most pleasant and memorable days in the history of the Corps.

Early in July the Canadian Corps was ordered to relieve the XVII Corps astride the Scarpe, and the 4th Canadian Division took over the Gavrelle-Oppy sector on the morning of the 12th with two Brigades in line. Later the Third Brigade was put in line and our front extended to the Scarpe. The enemy was nervous at our reappearance in the line after the long period of rest, and evidently expected action on our part. This theory was fostered by a policy of vigorous patrolling and raids, together with gas-beam and artillery "strafes."

The situation on the Western Front in the middle of July was briefly as follows. The Germans had made no further effort on the Lys. At the end of May they had struck heavily and reached the Marne, capturing Soissons and Château Thierry. On June 9th they had attacked between Soissons and Montdidier at very heavy cost. This offensive had been continued against Chalons and Epernay, but with tremendous loss and little success.

The French and American attack on July 18th on the Soissons-Château Thierry front had smashed the German offensive, and the enemy accordingly retired to the Aisne, which materially shortened the Allied line.

At this stage the Allies were in a position to resume the offensive, and the plan for the relief of the pressure on the Amiens-Paris railway and the junction of the French and British Armies, which had been under consideration for some time, was considerably enlarged in scope, and its immediate execution was decided.

Surprise was essential to the success of the undertaking, and therefore every effort was made to maintain secrecy up to the last minute. In order to deceive the enemy a battalion from each of the 2nd and 3rd Canadian Divisions were put in the line near Ypres. Other steps were taken to advertise the presence of the Canadians in that area, while the units moving to the actual battle area entrained without knowing their destination.

The Division handed over the front at Oppy on the morning of August 2nd, and immediately commenced to move, entirely at night by train and bus, to a concentration area south-west of Amiens. Then commenced the approach march to the battle concentration positions near Boves Wood. As the nights were short and very dark and the marches long, this period entailed considerable hardships for the troops and also the supply organization. However, the Division was concentrated near Boves Wood at dawn on the 7th without serious mishap, and in Gentelles Wood by dawn on the 8th.

At 4.20 a.m. on the 8th the 3rd Canadian Division on the right, the 1st Canadian Division in the centre, and the 2nd Canadian Division on the left, together with the First French Army on the right and the Australian Corps on the left, commenced the attack. The 4th Canadian Division followed the 3rd Canadian Division down the Roye Road, crossing the River Luce at Domart, and when the 3rd Canadian Division had taken their objective, the 4th Division lined up just short of the Mezieres-Cayeux Road, with the 11th Canadian Infantry Brigade on the right, the 12th Canadian Infantry Brigade on the left, and the 10th Canadian Infantry Brigade in reserve in the centre behind. Before our infantry jumped off at 12.10 p.m., the cavalry and some tanks had gone through, making for the " Blue Dotted Line," which was the old Amiens defence system of the pre-Somme days. The guns had shot themselves out over the 3rd Division, and therefore the only artillery support for our troops was that afforded by the few batteries which followed them along, coming into action only when the advance was held up.

The first real opposition came from Beaucourt Village, but this was overcome, and the advance continued to Beaucourt Wood, where very heavy machine-gun fire held up both the leading Brigades. Here a very gallant infantry attack finally cleared the situation up, and the line went forward once more. Considerable opposition was met and overcome by the left Brigade before they finally reached the " Blue Dotted Line." On the right the enemy was making a stout stand at Le Quesnel, and the fact that the French were not abreast of us on the right made the situation more difficult. However, before morning this village was taken, and the final objective was in our hands without causing any delay to the troops passing through.

This day the Division took the line forward from the 3rd Canadian Division, a distance of 6,000 yards on a 7,000-yard front.

On the 9th the 3rd Canadian Division and the 1st Canadian Division passed through us and continued the attack up to approximately the line Rouvroy-Meharicourt (inclusive).

Again, on the 10th, the 4th Canadian Division took up the battle on the line mentioned above, with the 10th Brigade on the right and the 12th Brigade on the left. Shortly after starting a maze of old wire and trenches was encountered, from which the enemy offered very determined resistance. With the aid of a few tanks, the line was taken forward to include Fouquescourt and Chilly. An entry was made into Hallu, but, owing to the situation on the flank, this was later abandoned.

After a short relief the Division again took over the line and consolidated the position, which was eventually handed over to the 34th and 35th French Divisions on August 25th, and the Division then moved back near Amiens. All ranks were struck by the businesslike methods of the French.

On August 26th came the news that Monchy-le-Preux had fallen, but few people in the Division dreamed that the 2nd and 3rd Canadian Divisions, who had only left us a few days before, had made the attack.

The Division commenced entraining at once, and by the 29th was concentrated near Arras. The line had been carried forward into territory which the Bosche had held since 1914, and this Division took it over just after the Fresnes-Rouvroy line had been captured. Our task was to take the Queant-Drocourt line, which was a portion of the famous Hindenburg system, and for which it was known that the enemy would make a desperate stand. The intention was to push through and make good the crossings of the Canal du Nord.

Considerable change in disposition was rendered necessary at a late hour, but the difficulties were overcome, and the Brigades formed up for the attack, with the 12th Canadian Infantry Brigade on the right, the 10th on the left, and the 11th in rear in reserve. From the time the leading Brigades took over the line right up to zero hour they were involved in almost continuous fighting, due to enemy counter-attacks and isolated posts of the enemy, which were calculated to hamper our jump-off.

At 5 a.m. on September 2nd the attack commenced. In spite of numerous German machine-gun nests inside our barrage, good progress was made, and by dint of stiff fighting in many places the Queant-Drocourt line was in our hands on time. Just beyond the last trench of this system the 11th Brigade and certain battalions of the other Brigades were to leap-frog and continue the advance, but the approach to the leap-frog line and the ground for a great distance beyond it was swept by terrific machine-gun fire from several angles. Our barrage had shot itself out in the first phase of the attack, and the only other weapons we had left were powerless to support further advance of the infantry under the circumstances. The second phase of the attack was therefore postponed till the next morning, but during the night the Huns retired to the far side of the Canal du Nord.

We followed them, and several villages fell into our hands, together with some forty French civilians who had been left in a cave in an unspeakable condition by the Bosche.

On the afternoon of the 3rd we pushed our posts well up to the western bank of the canal and dug in. The Bosche was on the far side, but seemed quite content to stay there. There were numerous efforts made to force a crossing of the canal, but none of them materialized, and in the end the Division was withdrawn on the 6th to the area between Cherisy and Arras, where it lived under most uninviting conditions, but managed to pull itself into shape once more to undertake the hardest fighting of its career in the Bourlon Wood and the subsequent operations.

Prior to the penetration of the Queant-Drocourt line the enemy had obviously decided to withdraw his disorganized armies from the Somme salient, and re-organize them behind the formidable Hindenburg Line. Part of this was now gone, but with the Canal du Nord as an extension of it there was still a chance of his effecting the re-organization. It was therefore imperative to continue the pressure. Further south the Canal du Nord had not been completed and contained no water, and it was decided to attempt a crossing at this place, in conjunction with the Third and Fourth Armies to our right.

Straight to our front lay the dominating Bourlon Wood, the loss of which in the autumn of 1917 had necessitated the withdrawal from most of the ground won by the Third Army.

The 4th Canadian Division on the right and the 1st Canadian Division on the left were to carry out the attack, with the 3rd Canadian Division and the 11th British Division ready to leap-frog them.

The concentration of the troops immediately prior to zero was a most difficult matter, as the available area was very restricted and filled with guns. Thanks in a large degree to the good work of the Engineers in building cross-country routes, all went well, and at 5.20 a.m. on September 27th the attack commenced.

The 10th Canadian Infantry Brigade advanced across the canal, the Canal du Nord Trench line, and up towards Bourlon Wood, where the fight was taken up by the 11th Canadian Infantry Brigade on the right and the 12th Canadian Infantry Brigade on the left. The advance on the left was hampered by heavy resistance during the afternoon, but the objective was eventually gained. On the right the plans for " pinching out " Bourlon Wood were spoiled and the situation seriously jeopardized by the failure of the troops on our right to get up. However, new plans were made on the spot, and the wood was taken and the line carried forward to the final objective. Severe counter-attacks from both flanks were beaten off and the line maintained intact.

Next morning the 3rd Canadian Division went through us on the right, and the 10th Canadian Infantry Brigade leap-frogged on the left and carried on the fight up to the Cambrai-Douai Road, where the resistance became very determined.

On the 29th and 30th the 12th and 11th Brigades

respectively attacked to push through to the Canal de l'Escaut and secure the crossings to Cambrai. In each case some initial headway was made, but the net gain in ground was small. The Germans were putting forth a terrific effort to maintain this ground.

On October 1st the 11th Brigade, with Canadian Divisions on either flank, again attacked. Once more good progress was made at first, but the Bosche held stoutly to Blecourt, and although troops of the 1st Canadian Division were at one time well beyond this village, it eventually remained in the hands of the enemy. Subsequent information showed that the enemy had put forth his every effort both in men and machine guns to hold this ground. Our front had now been swung round facing left, and although troops had got up almost to the canal, it was impossible to allow them to remain there. A line was dug in and handed over to the 2nd Canadian Division.

This closed the part of the 4th Canadian Division in the Battle of Cambrai—the hardest in its career. From the position gained other Canadian Divisions were able to capture Cambrai on the 9th. In the fighting from September 27th to October 1st the Division engaged and defeated no less than fifty-five German battalions, representing nine German Divisions. Approximately 2,000 prisoners were taken.

The Division was then withdrawn to the Inchy-Queant area to train and refit, and later to the Haute Avesnes-Arras area.

In the meantime the Third and Fourth Armies had passed the Hindenburg Line at every point, and there was no organized defence behind which the Germans could rally. They were falling back everywhere, and had now evacuated the Lys Salient and a portion of the ground east and south of Lens; but they were still holding a line west of Lille-Douai and along the Canal de la Sensee.

The Canadian Corps was now switched to a new front on the Canal de la Sensee south of Douai. The 4th

Canadian Division took over the line abreast of Aubigny-au-Bac from the 56th Division on October 16th. On the 17th, by sending a Battalion across on the 1st Canadian Division's front to work down the far side of the Canal, almost the whole Division got over and started in pursuit of the retreating Hun.

Although the enemy was carrying out a general retirement, his rearguard action was well fought, and considerable platoon manœuvre was necessary in order to continue the advance. This resistance gradually stiffened as we drew closer to the Canal de l'Escaut.

A new policy was now adopted in the employment of the Canadian Motor Machine Gun Brigade, who during the Battles of Amiens and Cambrai had operated as an independent force. The armoured cars and guns had been most ably handled by the gunners and crews, but at the same time, in so far as this division was concerned, the full benefit of their tremendous power had not been secured by the means then employed. They created too great a congestion upon the roads and areas over which the infantry were obliged to pass, and by their continual movement up and down these roads drew fire on the infantry without producing proportionate assistance. Application was therefore made to the Corps Commander for permission to have detached to this Division a certain number of armoured cars with guns. These, in turn, were placed at the disposal of the Brigades in the attack, and directly under Battalion Commanders. By this means very great assistance was obtained. They were in continuous touch with the operations in hand, and in close liaison with the Officer immediately in charge of the operation. They were thus enabled to circulate on various roads, and outflank small machine-gun nests and positions which had been holding up the infantry, causing considerable casualties to the enemy, and assisting our advances. So great was their power in this respect that in all our subsequent operations they were employed in this manner with most satisfactory results.

The work of demolition had been very effectively carried out. All bridges were down, water-levels had been altered, large craters were blown at all crossroads, every rail on the lines had been blown out, telegraph poles were cut down, mining machinery smashed, and, in short, every conceivable thing had been done to lay waste the country and impede our progress. In consequence, the work thrown upon the Engineers was colossal, but it was cheerfully undertaken and quickly executed. The much-despised pontoon came into its own, and, indeed, all arms were clamouring for more bridges.

Remarkable as the accomplishments of the Sappers were, there still remained tremendous difficulties in the way of all transportation. The consequent strain on the Divisional Ammunition Column and the Divisional Train was enormous, but here, again, it was cheerfully met, and the operating troops never went short. The situation was not improved by having to feed some 40,000 French civilians whom the Division delivered during the advance. This made three times the number of persons normally supplied by the Divisional Train.

The first hold-up of any importance occurred at Denain. Our progress was much hampered by our inability to employ artillery against the Bosche as he was taking cover behind the skirts of the civilians. However, the town was taken on the evening of the 20th.

By the 22nd the Division had worked its way forward to the Canal, which formed at the same time our southern boundary and front line. Our troops were looking out across the broad floods of the Canal at Valenciennes to our front and the commanding ground to our right front, topped by Mount Houy.

Attempts were made to cross the floods, but the Bosche resistance was too strong. In the meantime the XXII Corps to our right was attempting to take Mount Houy and thus clear Valenciennes from the south. They made several attempts, but in their weakened condition little progress was made.

The 4th Canadian Division was then given the job, and accordingly the 10th Canadian Infantry Brigade relieved the XXII Corps in the section immediately south of the Canal on October 29th-30th. On November 1st they attacked, took Mount Houy, and went forward to the southern outskirts of Valenciennes. This was a particularly brilliant achievement, and the more so in view of our decision not to shell Valenciennes and the villages to the south where civilians were known to have been left by the Germans. The prisoners taken by the 10th Brigade (1,800) exceeded the number of assaulting troops, and in addition 800 Germans were buried by them.

In the evening troops of the 12th Canadian Infantry Brigade had worked across the Canal on their front, and next day they, with the 11th Canadian Infantry Brigade, who had gone through the 10th Canadian Infantry Brigade, cleared the city of Valenciennes.

For the next few days these two Brigades continued the advance in face of very stubborn resistance by the enemy. Good progress was made along the Mons road, and on the 5th our troops crossed the Aunelle River by a brilliant manœuvre, and were thus on Belgian territory.

The way to Mons had been laid open, and other Canadian Divisions which took over from us the next night entered the famous city a few hours before the Armistice came into effect on the morning of November 11th. The Division then withdrew to the Valenciennes area, having completed its last battle tour in the Great War.

A few days later we moved to the Mons area, where preparations were made in anticipation for the march to the Rhine. Owing to the extreme difficulties with transportation, the number of Canadian divisions for the Rhine was subsequently reduced to two, which ruled this Division out.

Shortly afterwards the Division moved to an area mid-way between Brussels and Huy, and later to the Wavre-Waterloo-Boitfort area, some 10 miles south of

Brussels. The winter was occupied chiefly in athletics and educational training, with frequent trips to the many places of interest in and around the Belgian capital.

On April 14th the Division commenced its move to Havre preparatory to demobilization. By May 10th the whole Division was concentrated in Bramshott Camp, Hants.

Representative troops of the whole Division took part in the parade of the Dominion troops through London on May 3rd, when they were accorded a welcome that will long be remembered by all who were present.

This was indeed a fitting close to the career of the Division before it embarked for Canada towards the end of May.

BATTLE ORDER OF 4th CANADIAN DIVISION
(1/8/16).

DIVISIONAL HEADQUARTERS.
General Officer Commanding.
Major-General David Watson, C.M.G.
Aides-de-Camp.
(1) Capt. G. L. Boyer.　　(2) Capt. H. F. Hall.
(3) Capt. R. M. Redmond.
General Staff Officer I.
Lieut.-Col. W. E. Ironside, D.S.O.
General Staff Officer II.
Major D. K. B. Murray, D.S.O.
General Staff Officer II.
Major A. G. Turner, M.C.
General Staff Officer III.
Major G. G. Morriss.
General Staff Officer III.
Captain A. A. Aitken.
A.A. and Q.M.G.
Lieut.-Col. E. de B. Panet, D.S.O.
D.A.A. and Q.M.G.
Major H. C. Greer.
D.A.Q.M.G.
Captain F. R. Burnside, D.S.O.
D.A.A.G.
Captain C. A. Moorhead.
A.P.M.
Major J. F. Foulkes.
A.D.M.S.
Lieut.-Col. H. A. Chisholm.
D.A.D.M.S.
Major J. S. Jenkins.
A.D.V.S.
Major C. E. Edgett.
D.A.D.O.S.
Captain G. Spindler.
Senior Chaplain.
Major A. M. Gordon, M.C.
Field Cashier.
Major S. R. Heakes.
Divisional Claims Officer.
Major L. H. Webber.

Battle Order (1/8/16)—*Continued.*

10TH CANADIAN INFANTRY BRIGADE.

General Officer Commanding.
Brigadier-General W. St. P. Hughes.

Orderly Officer.
Lieutenant C. J. Tidmarsh.

Brigade Major.
Captain V. B. Ramsden, M.C.

Staff Captain (I).	*Staff Captain (Q).*
Captain C. T. Macklem.	Captain J. S. Gzowski.

44TH CANADIAN INFANTRY BATTALION.

Officer Commanding.	*Adjutant.*
Lieut.-Col. E. R. Wayland.	Captain G. W. McFarlane.

46TH CANADIAN INFANTRY BATTALION.

Officer Commanding.	*Adjutant.*
Lieut.-Col. H. J. Dawson.	Captain J. A. Dann.

47TH CANADIAN INFANTRY BATTALION.

Officer Commanding.	*Adjutant.*
Lieut.-Col. W. N. Winsby.	Major C. Carmichael.

50TH CANADIAN INFANTRY BATTALION.

Officer Commanding.	*Adjutant.*
Lieut.-Col. E. G. Mason.	Captain J. S. Wright.

10TH CANADIAN MACHINE GUN COMPANY.

Officer Commanding.
Lieutenant C. F. Bowring.

10TH CANADIAN LIGHT TRENCH MORTAR BATTERY.

Officer Commanding.
Captain H. K. Clemens.

BATTLE ORDER (1/8/16)—*Continued*.

11TH CANADIAN INFANTRY BRIGADE.

General Officer Commanding.
Brigadier-General V. W. Odlum, D.S.O.

Orderly Officer.
Captain G. Paterson.

Brigade Major.
Captain R. J. A. Henniker.

Staff Captain (I).	*Staff Captain (Q).*
Major N. D. Perry.	Captain F. R. Phelan.

54TH CANADIAN INFANTRY BATTALION.

Officer Commanding.	*Adjutant.*
Lieut.-Col. A. H. G. Kemball, C.B., D.S.O.	Lieut. R. A. Holmes à-Court.

75TH CANADIAN INFANTRY BATTALION.

Officer Commanding.	*Adjutant.*
Lieut.-Col. S. G. Beckett.	Captain J. M. Langstaff.

87TH CANADIAN INFANTRY BATTALION.

Officer Commanding.	*Adjutant.*
Lieut.-Col. R. W. Frost.	Captain W. M. Kirkpatrick.

102ND CANADIAN INFANTRY BATTALION.

Officer Commanding.	*Adjutant.*
Lieut.-Col. J. W. Warden.	Captain H. B. Scharschmidt.

11TH CANADIAN MACHINE GUN COMPANY.

Officer Commanding.
Major B. M. Clerk.

11TH CANADIAN LIGHT TRENCH MORTAR BATTERY.

Officer Commanding.
Captain F. J. O'Leary.

BATTLE ORDER (1/8/16)—*Continued.*

12TH CANADIAN INFANTRY BRIGADE.

General Officer Commanding.
Brigadier-General Lord Brooke, C.M.G., M.V.O.

Orderly Officer.
Captain E. Bassett.

Brigade Major.
Major R. E. Partridge.

Staff Captain (I).	*Staff Captain (Q).*
Captain W. Neilson.	Captain K. R. Marshall.

38TH CANADIAN INFANTRY BATTALION.

Officer Commanding.	*Adjutant.*
Lieut.-Col. C. M. Edwards.	Captain J. Glass.

73RD CANADIAN INFANTRY BATTALION. (REPLACED BY 85TH CANADIAN INFANTRY BATTALION, FEBRUARY, 1917.)

Officer Commanding.	*Adjutant.*
Lieut.-Col. Peers Davidson.	Captain H. W. Morgan.

72ND CANADIAN INFANTRY BATTALION.

Officer Commanding.	*Adjutant.*
Lieut.-Col. J. A. Clarke.	Major D. D. Young.

78TH CANADIAN INFANTRY BATTALION.

Officer Commanding.	*Adjutant.*
Lieut.-Col. J. Kirkaldy.	Captain F. W. Goossens.

12TH CANADIAN MACHINE GUN COMPANY.

Officer Commanding.
Captain H. E. Hodge.

12TH CANADIAN LIGHT TRENCH MORTAR BATTERY.

Officer Commanding.
Captain A. Leighton.

BATTLE ORDER (1/8/16)—*Continued.*

Commanding Royal Engineers.
Lieut.-Col. G. A. Inksetter.

10th Field Company, Canadian Engineers. *Officer Commanding :*
Major W. P. Wilgar.

11th Field Company, Canadian Engineers. *Officer Commanding :*
Major H. L. Trotter.

12th Field Company, Canadian Engineers. *Officer Commanding :*
Major C. T. Trotter.

67TH CANADIAN PIONEER BATTALION. (REPLACED BY 124TH CANADIAN PIONEER BATTALION, MARCH, 1917.)

Officer Commanding.	*Adjutant.*
Lieut.-Col. L. Ross.	Major C. C. Harbottle.

4TH CANADIAN DIVISIONAL SIGNAL COMPANY.
Officer Commanding.
Major A. G. Lawson.

4TH CANADIAN DIVISIONAL TRAIN.
Officer Commanding.
Lieut.-Col. R. H. Webb, M.C.

11TH FIELD AMBULANCE, C.A.M.C.
Officer Commanding.
Lieut.-Col. J. D. McQueen.

12TH FIELD AMBULANCE, C.A.M.C.
Officer Commanding.
Lieut.-Col. H. F. Gordon.

13TH FIELD AMBULANCE, C.A.M.C.
Officer Commanding.
Lieut.-Col. J. L. Biggar.

BATTLE ORDER OF 4th CANADIAN DIVISION (1/8/17).

DIVISIONAL HEADQUARTERS.

General Officer Commanding.
Major-General David Watson, C.M.G.

Aides-de-Camp.
(1) Captain H. W. Walker.   (2) Captain R. M. Redmond.
(3) Lieutenant P. L. A. Garneau.

General Staff Officer I.
Lieut.-Col. W. E. Ironside, C.M.G., D.S.O.

General Staff Officer II.
Major Hon. T. G. B. Morgan-Grenville-Gavin, M.C.

General Staff Officer II.
Major A. G. Turner, M.C.

General Staff Officer III.
Major N. D. Perry.

General Staff Officer III.
Captain A. A. Aitken.

A.A. and Q.M.G.
Lieut.-Col. E. de B. Panet, D.S.O.

D.A.Q.M.G.
Captain D. H. Barnett, M.C.

D.A.A.G.
Major N. O. Reiffenstein.

D.A.A.G.
Major A. E. Taylor.

A.P.M.
Major J. F. Foulkes.

A.D.M.S.
Colonel C. A. Peters, D.S.O.

D.A.D.M.S.
Major J. S. Jenkins, D.S.O.

A.D.V.S.
Lieut.-Col. C. E. Edgett.

D.A.D.O.S.
Captain J. Larkin.

Senior Chaplain.
Major A. M. Gordon, M.C.

Field Cashier.
Major S. R. Heakes.

Divisional Claims Officer.
Lieutenant J. R. Wallace.

BATTLE ORDER (1/8/17)—*Continued.*

10TH CANADIAN INFANTRY BRIGADE.

General Officer Commanding.
Brigadier-General E. Hilliam, D.S.O.

Orderly Officer.
Lieutenant L. W. G. Meikle.

Brigade Major.
Captain R. V. Read.

Staff Captain (I).	*Staff Captain (Q).*
Captain E. H. Hill.	Major D. J. O'Donahoe.

44TH CANADIAN INFANTRY BATTALION.
Officer Commanding.	*Adjutant.*
Lieut.-Col. R. D. Davies, D.S.O.	Captain R. R. Brough, M.C.

46TH CANADIAN INFANTRY BATTALION.
Officer Commanding.	*Adjutant.*
Lieut.-Col. H. J. Dawson, D.S.O.	Major J. A. Hope, M.C.

47TH CANADIAN INFANTRY BATTALION.
Officer Commanding.	*Adjutant.*
Lieut.-Col. M. J. Francis.	Major C. Carmichael.

50TH CANADIAN INFANTRY BATTALION.
Officer Commanding.	*Adjutant.*
Lieut.-Col. L. F. Page, D.S.O.	Major H. L. Keegan.

10TH CANADIAN MACHINE GUN COMPANY. (ABSORBED INTO 4TH BATTALION CANADIAN MACHINE GUN CORPS, 22/2/18.)

Officer Commanding.
Major J. C. Britton.

10TH CANADIAN LIGHT TRENCH MORTAR BATTERY.
Officer Commanding.
Captain R. W. Course.

31

BATTLE ORDER (1/8/17)—*Continued.*

11TH CANADIAN INFANTRY BRIGADE.

General Officer Commanding.
Brigadier-General V. W. Odlum, C.M.G., D.S.O.
Orderly Officer.
Lieutenant W. S. McCann.
Brigade Major.
Major W. H. Collum, M.C.

Staff Captain (I).	*Staff Captain (Q).*
Captain E. O. C. Martin.	Captain F. R. Phelan.

54TH CANADIAN INFANTRY BATTALION.

Officer Commanding.	*Adjutant.*
Lieut.-Col. A. B. Carey, D.S.O.	Major T. E. L. Taylor.

75TH CANADIAN INFANTRY BATTALION.

Officer Commanding.	*Adjutant.*
Lieut.-Col. C. C. Harbottle.	Captain A. A. Gray.

87TH CANADIAN INFANTRY BATTALION.

Officer Commanding.	*Adjutant.*
Lieut.-Col. J. V. P. O'Donahoe, D.S.O.	Captain W. M. Kirkpatrick.

102ND CANADIAN INFANTRY BATTALION.

Officer Commanding.	*Adjutant.*
Lieut.-Col. J. W. Warden, D.S.O.	Captain S. H. O'Kell.

11TH CANADIAN MACHINE GUN COMPANY. (ABSORBED INTO 4TH BATTALION CANADIAN MACHINE GUN CORPS, 22/2/18.)

Officer Commanding.
Major B. M. Clerk, M.C.

11TH CANADIAN LIGHT TRENCH MORTAR BATTERY.

Officer Commanding.
Captain A. Black.

BATTLE ORDER (1/8/17)—*Continued.*

12TH CANADIAN INFANTRY BRIGADE.

General Officer Commanding.
Brigadier-General J. H. MacBrien, C.M.G., D.S.O.
Orderly Officer.
Lieutenant G. Roberts, M.C.
Brigade Major.
Lieut.-Col. H. C. Sparling, D.S.O.

Staff Captain (I).	*Staff Captain (Q).*
Major S. D. Armour.	Captain J. M. Pauline, M.C.

38TH CANADIAN INFANTRY BATTALION.

Officer Commanding.	*Adjutant.*
Lieut.-Col. C. M. Edwards, D.S.O.	Captain J. O. Slagt, M.C.

72ND CANADIAN INFANTRY BATTALION.

Officer Commanding.	*Adjutant.*
Lieut.-Col. J. A. Clarke, D.S.O.	Captain A. P. Foster.

78TH CANADIAN INFANTRY BATTALION.

Officer Commanding.	*Adjutant.*
Lieut.-Col. J. Kirkcaldy, D.S.O.	Major F. D. Scruton.

85TH CANADIAN INFANTRY BATTALION.

Officer Commanding.	*Adjutant.*
Lieut.-Col. A. H. Borden.	Major J. L. Ralston.

12TH CANADIAN MACHINE GUN COMPANY. (ABSORBED INTO 4TH BATTALION CANADIAN MACHINE GUN CORPS, 22/2/18.)

Officer Commanding.
Major L. F. Pearce, M.C.

12TH CANADIAN LIGHT TRENCH MORTAR BATTERY.

Officer Commanding.
Captain H. S. Pedley.

BATTLE ORDER (1/8/17)—*Continued.*

4TH CANADIAN DIVISIONAL ARTILLERY.

Commanding Royal Artillery.
Brigadier-General C. H. MacLaren, D.S.O.

Brigade Major.
Major L. C. Goodeve, D.S.O.

Staff Captain.
Captain J. O'Reilly.

Staff Captain.
Captain E. B. Savage.

Divisional Trench Mortar Officer.
Captain G. H. Davidson.

Reconnaissance Officer.
Lieutenant P. H. Wright.

3RD BRIGADE CANADIAN FIELD ARTILLERY.
(TRANSFERRED FROM 1ST CANADIAN DIVISIONAL ARTILLERY.)

Officer Commanding.	*Adjutant.*
Major J. A. MacDonald.	Lieutenant R. T. Smith

4TH BRIGADE CANADIAN FIELD ARTILLERY.
(TRANSFERRED FROM 2ND CANADIAN DIVISIONAL ARTILLERY.)

Officer Commanding.	*Adjutant.*
Lieut.-Col. J. S. Stewart, D.S.O.	Lieutenant M. O'Halloran.

4TH CANADIAN DIVISIONAL AMMUNITION COLUMN.
(RE-FORMED IN FRANCE FROM 1ST, 2ND, AND 3RD CANADIAN DIVISIONS.)

Officer Commanding.	*Adjutant.*
Major E. T. B. Gillmore.	Lieutenant R. M. Haultain.

16TH CANADIAN MACHINE GUN COMPANY. (ABSORBED INTO 4TH BATTALION CANADIAN MACHINE GUN CORPS, 22/2/18.)

Officer Commanding.
Captain E. W. Sansom.

BATTLE ORDER (1/8/17)—*Continued.*

Commanding Royal Engineers.

Lieut.-Col. T. C. Irving, D.S.O.

10th Field Company Canadian Engineers. *Officer Commanding :*
Major W. P. Wilgar, D S.O.

11th Field Company Canadian Engineers. *Officer Commanding :*
Major H. L. Trotter.

12th Field Company Canadian Engineers. *Officer Commanding :*
Major E. J. C. Schmidlin, M.C.

124TH CANADIAN PIONEER BATTALION.

Officer Commanding. *Adjutant.*

Lieut.-Col. W. C. V. Chadwick. Captain R. C. Berkinshaw.

(10th, 11th, and 12th Field Companies Canadian Engineers, and 124th Canadian Pioneer Battalion, absorbed into 4th Brigade Canadian Engineers, 24/5/18.)

4TH CANADIAN DIVISIONAL SIGNAL COMPANY.
Officer Commanding.
Major A. G. Lawson, M.C.

4TH CANADIAN DIVISIONAL TRAIN.
Officer Commanding.
Lieut.-Col. R. H. Webb, D.S.O., M.C.

11TH FIELD AMBULANCE, C.A.M.C.
Officer Commanding.
Lieut.-Col. H. H. Moshier.

12TH FIELD AMBULANCE, C.A.M.C.
Officer Commanding.
Lieut.-Col. P. G. Bell. D.S.O.

13TH FIELD AMBULANCE, C.A.M.C.
Officer Commanding.
Lieut.-Col. A. C. L. Gilday, D.S.O.

BATTLE ORDER OF 4th CANADIAN DIVISION
(1/8/18.)

DIVISIONAL HEADQUARTERS.

General Officer Commanding.
Major-General Sir David Watson, K.C.B., C.M.G.

Aides-de-Camp.
(1) Capt. H. W. Walker. (2) Lieut. P. L. A. Garneau.
(3) Capt. W. McLeod Moore. (4) Lieut. N. D. Ayer.

General Staff Officer I.
Lieut.-Col. E. de B. Panet, C.M.G., D.S.O.

General Staff Officer II.
Major Hon. T. G. B. Morgan-Grenville-Gavin, D.S.O., M.C.

General Staff Officer II.
Lieut.-Col. A. A. McGee.

General Staff Officer III.
Major J. E. Hahn, M.C.

General Staff Officer III.
Major S. D. Armour.

A.A. and Q.M.G.
Lieut.-Col. K. R. Marshall, D.S.O.

D.A.Q.M.G.
Major A. E. Taylor, D.S.O.

D.A.A.G.
Major G. S. Currie, M.C.

D.A.A.G.
Captain J. M. Pauline, M.C.

A.P.M.
Major J. F. Foulkes.

A.D.M.S.
Colonel C. A. Peters, D.S.O.

D.A.D.M.S.
Major G. Garnett Greer, M.C.

D.A.D.V.S.
Major W. G. Stedman.

D.A.D.O.S.
Major H. A. T. Bennett.

Senior Chaplain.
Lieut.-Col .A. M. Gordon, M.C.

Field Cashier.
Major C. W. Ward.

Divisional Claims Officer.
Lieutenant J. R. Wallace.

BATTLE ORDER (1/8/18)—*Continued.*

10TH CANADIAN INFANTRY BRIGADE.

General Officer Commanding.
Brigadier-General R. J. F. Hayter, C.M.G., D.S.O.

Orderly Officer.
Lieutenant H. Y. Hicking.

Brigade Major.
Major N. D. Perry, D.S.O.

Staff Captain (I).   *Staff Captain (Q).*
Lieut. A. J. Everett, M.C.   Major D. J. O'Donahoe, D.S O.

44TH CANADIAN INFANTRY BATTALION.

Officer Commanding.   *Adjutant.*
Lieut.-Col. R. D. Davies, D.S O.   Lieutenant J. B. Gould

46TH CANADIAN INFANTRY BATTALION.

Officer Commanding.   *Adjutant.*
Lieut.-Col. H. J. Dawson, D.S.O.   Captain S. Lett.

47TH CANADIAN INFANTRY BATTALION.

Officer Commanding.   *Adjutant.*
Lieut.-Col. H. L. Keegan, D.S.O.   Captain W. H. Allsopp.

50TH CANADIAN INFANTRY BATTALION.

Officer Commanding.   *Adjutant.*
Lt.-Col. L. F. Page, D.S.O.   Captain T. H. Prescott, M.C.

10TH CANADIAN LIGHT TRENCH MORTAR BATTERY
(Disbanded after Armistice, 11/11/18).

Officer Commanding.
Captain F. C. Ross.

BATTLE ORDER (1/8/18)—*Continued.*

11TH CANADIAN INFANTRY BRIGADE.

General Officer Commanding.
Brigadier-General V. W. Odlum. C.M.G., D.S.O.

Brigade Major.
Major C. B. Lindsey, D.S.O.

Staff Captain (I).   *Staff Captain (Q).*
Captain W. S. McCann, M.C.   Captain R. H. Richardson, M.C.

54TH CANADIAN INFANTRY BATTALION.

Officer Commanding.   *Adjutant.*
Lieut.-Col. A. B. Carey, D.S.O.   Captain W. G. Foster.

75TH CANADIAN INFANTRY BATTALION.

Officer Commanding.   *Adjutant.*
Lieut.-Col. C. C. Harbottle, D.S.O.   Captain F. K. Prouse, M.C.

87TH CANADIAN INFANTRY BATTALION.

Officer Commanding.   *Adjutant.*
Lieut.-Col. K. M. Perry, D.S.O.   Captain L. W. W. Slack, M.C.

102ND CANADIAN INFANTRY BATTALION.

Officer Commanding.   *Adjutant.*
Lieut.-Col. F. Lister, D.S.O., M.C.   Captain S. H. O'Kell.

11TH CANADIAN LIGHT TRENCH MORTAR BATTERY
(Disbanded after Armistice, 11/11/18).

Officer Commanding.
Captain A. Black, M.C.

BATTLE ORDER (1/8/18)—*Continued*.

12TH CANADIAN INFANTRY BRIGADE.

General Officer Commanding.
Brigadier-General J. H. MacBrien, C.M.G., D.S.O.

Orderly Officer.
Lieutenant W. A. H. MacBrien.

Brigade Major.
Major T. P. Jones, D.S.O.

Staff Captain (I).   *Staff Captain (Q).*
Capt. W. C. Merston, M.C., D.C.M.   Capt. V. N. Smallpiece.

38TH CANADIAN INFANTRY BATTALION.

Officer Commanding.   *Adjutant.*
Lieut.-Col. C. M. Edwards, D.S.O.   Captain L. F. Goodwin, M.C.

72ND CANADIAN INFANTRY BATTALION.

Officer Commanding.   *Adjutant.*
Lieut.-Col. G. H. Kirkpatrick.   Captain W. G. McIntosh.

78TH CANADIAN INFANTRY BATTALION.

Officer Commanding.   *Adjutant.*
Lieut.-Col. J. Kirkcaldy, D.S.O.   Captain S. J. Cragg.

85TH CANADIAN INFANTRY BATTALION.

Officer Commanding.   *Adjutant.*
Lieut.-Col. J. L. Ralston, D.S.O.   Captain A. T. Croft.

12TH CANADIAN TRENCH LIGHT MORTAR BATTERY
(Disbanded after Armistice, 11/11/18).

Officer Commanding.
Captain S. G. McKenzie.

BATTLE ORDER (1/8/18)—*Continued.*

4TH CANADIAN DIVISIONAL ARTILLERY.

Commanding Royal Artillery.
Brigadier-General W. B. M. King, C.M.G., D.S.O.

Brigade Major.
Major L. C. Goodeve, D.S.O.

Staff Captain.   *Staff Captain.*
Captain J. O'Reilly.   Captain E. B. Savage, M.C.

Divisional Trench Mortar Officer.
Captain G. H. Davidson, M.C.

Reconnaissance Officer.
Lieutenant H. L. McPherson, M.C.

3RD BRIGADE CANADIAN FIELD ARTILLERY.

Officer Commanding.   *Adjutant.*
Lieut.-Col. J. A. McDonald, D.S.O.   Lieutenant D. W. Ferrier, M.C.

4TH BRIGADE CANADIAN FIELD ARTILLERY.
Officer Commanding.   *Adjutant.*
Lieut.-Col. M. N. Ross, D.S.O.   Lieutenant H. W. Larkin, M.C.

4TH CANADIAN DIVISIONAL AMMUNITION COLUMN.
Officer Commanding.   *Adjutant.*
Lt.-Col. E. T. B. Gillmore, D.S.O.   Lieut. T. H. Atkinson, M.C.

BATTLE ORDER (1/8/18)—*Continued.*

4TH BRIGADE CANADIAN ENGINEERS.

Commanding Royal Engineers.
Colonel H. T. Hughes, C.M.G.

Brigade Major.
Major M. A. Pope, M.C.

| *Staff Captain.* | *Staff Captain.* |

Captain R. D. Sutherland, M.C. Captain F. R. Alport, M.C.

10TH BATTALION CANADIAN ENGINEERS.
Officer Commanding.
Lieut.-Col. W. P. Wilgar, D.S.O.

11TH BATTALION CANADIAN ENGINEERS.
Officer Commanding.
Lieut.-Col. H. L. Trotter, D.S.O.

12TH BATTALION CANADIAN ENGINEERS.
Officer Commanding.
Lieut.-Col. J. T. C. Thompson.

4TH BN. CANADIAN MACHINE GUN CORPS.

| *Officer Commanding.* | *Adjutant.* |

Lieut.-Col. M. A. Scott, D.S.O. Captain H. Ward, M.C.

4TH CANADIAN DIVISIONAL SIGNAL COMPANY.

Officer Commanding.
Major F. G. Malloch, M.C.

4TH CANADIAN DIVISIONAL TRAIN.

Officer Commanding.
Lieut.-Col. W. D. Greer, D.S.O.

11TH FIELD AMBULANCE, C.A.M.C.
Officer Commanding.
Lieut.-Col. H. H. Moshier.

12TH FIELD AMBULANCE, C.A.M.C.
Officer Commanding.
Lieut.-Col. P. G. Bell, D.S.O.

13TH FIELD AMBULANCE, C.A.M.C.
Officer Commanding.
Lieut.-Col. W. H. K. Anderson, D.S.O.

BATTLE ORDER OF 4th CANADIAN DIVISION (8/3/19).

DIVISIONAL HEADQUARTERS.

General Officer Commanding.
Major-General Sir David Watson, K.C.B., C.M.G.
Aides-de-Camp.
(1) Captain J. R. Wallace.　　(2) Captain H. Y. Hicking.
General Staff Officer (I).
Lieut.-Col. T. M. McAvity, D.S.O.
General Staff Officer (II).
Major Hon. F. E. Grosvenor, D.S.O., M.C.
General Staff Officer (II).
Major C. B. Lindsey, D.S.O.
General Staff Officer (III).
Major S. D. Armour.
General Staff Officer (III).
Captain W. C. Merston, M.C., D.C.M.
A.A. and Q.M.G.
Lieut.-Col. K. R. Marshall, C.M.G., D.S.O.
D.A.Q.M.G.
Major G. S. Currie, D.S.O., M.C.
D.A.A.G.
Major D. J. O'Donahoe, D.S.O.
D.A.A.G.
Major J. O'Reilly.
A.P.M.
Major J. F. Foulkes, D.S.O.
A.D.M.S.
Colonel P. G. Bell, D.S.O.
D.A.D.M.S.
Major J. C. Maynard.
D.A.D.V.S.
Major W. G. Stedman.
D.A.D.O.S.
Major H. A. T. Bennett.
Senior Chaplain.
Major A. P. Shatford.
Field Cashier.
Major H. Hill, O.B.E.
Divisional Claims Officer.
Lieut.-Col. Sir H. Montague Allan, KNT., C.V.O.

BATTLE ORDER (8/3/19)—*Continued.*

10TH CANADIAN INFANTRY BRIGADE

General Officer Commanding.
Brigadier-General J. M. Ross, C.M.G., D.S.O.

Brigade Major.
Major N. D. Perry, D.S.O.

Staff Captain (I).   *Staff Captain (Q).*
Major W. O. White, M.C.   Captain A. C. M. Thomson, M.C.

44TH CANADIAN INFANTRY BATTALION.

Officer Commanding.   *Adjutant.*
Lieut.-Col. R. D. Davies, D.S.O.   Captain A. R. Ross, M.C.

46TH CANADIAN INFANTRY BATTALION.

Officer Commanding.   *Adjutant.*
Lieut.-Col. H. J. Dawson, C.M.G., D.S.O.   Captain S. Leet.

47TH CANADIAN INFANTRY BATTALION.

Officer Commanding.   *Adjutant.*
Lieut.-Col. H. L. Keegan, D.S.O.   Lieut. W. H. Lindsell, M C.

50TH CANADIAN INFANTRY BATTALION.

Officer Commanding.   *Adjutant.*
Lieut.-Col. L. F. Page, D.S.O.   Captain T. H. Prescott, MC.

BATTLE ORDER (8/3/19)—*Continued.*

11TH CANADIAN INFANTRY BRIGADE.

General Officer Commanding.
Brigadier-General V. W. Odlum, C.B., C.M.G., D.S.O.

Orderly Officer.
Lieutenant J. C. Mitchell, M.C.

Brigade Major.
Major J. E. Hahn, M.C.

Staff Captain (I).   *Staff Captain (Q).*
Capt. D. S. Montgomery, M.C.   Capt. H. W. Walker, M.C.

54TH CANADIAN INFANTRY BATTALION.

Officer Commanding.   *Adjutant.*
Lieut.-Col. A. B. Carey, D.S.O.   Captain V. P. Peat.

75TH CANADIAN INFANTRY BATTALION.

Officer Commanding.   *Adjutant.*
Lieut.-Col. C. C. Harbottle, D.S.O.   Captain A. A. Gray, M.C.

87TH CANADIAN INFANTRY BATTALION.

Officer Commanding.   *Adjutant.*
Lieut.-Col. R. Bickerdike, D.S.O.   Captain G. S. Stairs, M.C.

102ND CANADIAN INFANTRY BATTALION.

Officer Commanding.   *Adjutant.*
Lieut.-Col. F. Lister, D.S.O., M.C.   Captain W. W. Dunlop, M.C.

BATTLE ORDER (8/3/19)—*Continued*.

12TH CANADIAN INFANTRY BRIGADE.

General Officer Commanding.
Brigadier-General J. Kirkcaldy, D.S.O.

Orderly Officer.
Lieutenant W. A. H. MacBrien.

Brigade Major.
Major T. P. Jones, D.S.O.

Staff Captain (I).   *Staff Captain (Q).*
Captain E. L. M. Burns, M.C.   Captain V. N. Smallpiece, M.C.

38TH CANADIAN INFANTRY BATTALION.
Officer Commanding.   *Adjutant.*
Lieut.-Col. A. D. Cameron, M.C.   Captain J. C. Cooke, M.C.

72ND CANADIAN INFANTRY BATTALION.
Officer Commanding.   *Adjutant.*
Lieut.-Col. G. H. Kirkpatrick, D.S.O.   Captain S. R. Say.

78TH CANADIAN INFANTRY BATTALION.
Officer Commanding.   *Adjutant.*
Lieut.-Col. J. N. Semmens, D.S.O.   Captain L. P. Chalmers.

85TH CANADIAN INFANTRY BATTALION.
Officer Commanding.   *Adjutant.*
Lieut.-Col. J. L. Ralston, D.S.O.   Captain A. T. Croft.

BATTLE ORDER (8/3/19)—*Continued.*

4TH CANADIAN DIVISIONAL ARTILLERY.

Commanding Royal Artillery.
Brigadier-General W. B. M. King, C.M.G., D.S.O.

Brigade Major.
Major L. C. Goodeve, D.S.O.

Staff Captain.	*Staff Captain.*
Captain H. L. McPherson, M.C.	Lieutenant H. R. Case.

Divisional Trench Mortar Officer.
Captain G. H. Davidson, M.C.

Reconnaissance Officer.
Lieutenant D. W. Ferrier, M.C.

3RD BRIGADE CANADIAN FIELD ARTILLERY.

Officer Commanding.	*Adjutant.*
Lieut.-Col. J. A. McDonald, D.S.O.	Lieutenant J. Vickery.

4TH BRIGADE CANADIAN FIELD ARTILLERY.

Officer Commanding.	*Adjutant.*
Lieut.-Col. M. N. Ross, D.S.O.	Lieutenant H. W. Larkin, M.C.

4TH CANADIAN DIVISIONAL AMMUNITION COLUMN.

Officer Commanding.	*Adjutant.*
Lt.-Col. E. T. B. Gillmore, D.S.O.	Lieut. T. H. Atkinson, M.C.

BATTLE ORDER (8/3/19)—*Continued.*

4TH BRIGADE CANADIAN ENGINEERS.
Commanding Royal Engineers.
Colonel H. T. Hughes, C.M.G.
Brigade Major.
Major M. A. Pope, M.C.

Staff Captain.	*Staff Captain.*
Captain F. Alport, M.C.	Captain L. W. Klingner, M.C.

10TH BATTALION CANADIAN ENGINEERS.
Officer Commanding.
Lieut.-Col. W. P. Wilgar, D.S.O.

11TH BATTALION CANADIAN ENGINEERS.
Officer Commanding.
Lieut.-Col. H. L. Trotter, D.S.O.

12TH BATTALION CANADIAN ENGINEERS.
Officer Commanding.
Lieut.-Col. E. J. C. Schmidlin, M.C.

4TH BN. CANADIAN MACHINE GUN CORPS.

Officer Commanding.	*Adjutant.*
Lieut.-Col. M. A. Scott, D.S.O.	Captain H. Ward, M.C.

4TH CANADIAN DIVISIONAL SIGNAL COMPANY.
Officer Commanding.
Major F. G. Malloch, M.C.

4TH CANADIAN DIVISIONAL TRAIN.
Officer Commanding.
Lieut.-Col. W. D. Greer, D.S.O.

11TH FIELD AMBULANCE, C.A.M.C.
Officer Commanding.
Lieut.-Col. S. Paulin, D.S.O.

12TH FIELD AMBULANCE, C.A.M.C.
Officer Commanding.
Major E. A. Neff.

13TH FIELD AMBULANCE, C.A.M.C.
Officer Commanding.
Lieut.-Col. W. H. K. Anderson, D.S.O.

DATES OF INTEREST

1916.

August 10th ...	First troops embarked for France.
August 25th ...	Took over line from Ypres-Comines Canal to point opposite Messines.
September 23rd	Handed over line and started for the Somme.
September 23rd —October 3rd	Training at Tilques.
October 11th	Took over line in front of Regina Trench.
October 21st	Attack by 10th and 11th Brigades on Regina Trench.
October 25th	Attack by 44th Battalion on Regina Trench.
November 11th	10th Brigade completed capture of Regina Trench.
November 18th	Capture of Desire Trench.
November 28th	Handed over Somme line to 51st Division.
December 4th— December 18th	Refitting in Bruay-Divion area.
December 21st	Took over line on Vimy Ridge, immediately south of Souchez River.

1917.

March 1st ...	Gas attack by 11th and 12th Brigades.
April 9th ...	Attack on Vimy Ridge.
April 11th ...	Capture of " Pimple " by 10th Brigade.
April 13th ...	Line carried out on the flats east of Vimy Ridge.
April 14th ...	Division handed over line to 5th British Division, and moved to Château de la Haie area.
April 25th ...	Took over line between Vimy-Lens Railway and Souchez River.
June 5th ...	Capture of Central Electric Generating Station by 11th Canadian Infantry Brigade.
June 19th ...	Capture of the " Triangle."
June 26th ...	Capture of Brewery and La Coulotte.
June 28th ...	Capture of Eleu dit Leauvette by 12th Canadian Infantry Brigade.
July 2nd ...	Division moved to Barlin area.
July 20th ...	Divisional Sports at Barlin.
July 26th ...	Division took over line astride the Souchez River.

August 15th ...	Attack on the Green Crassier and Aconite Trench in co-operation with larger attack on Hill 70 to the north.
October 5th ...	Division started for Passchendaele.
October 22nd	10th Brigade took over line, and Division takes over from 3rd Australian Division.
October 26th...	10th Canadian Infantry Brigade attack line Haalen Copse-Decline Copse.
October 30th	12th Canadian Infantry Brigade captured line Tiber Copse-Crest Farm.
November 3rd	Handed over line to 2nd Canadian Division, and withdrew to Caestre area.
November 12th	Division again took over the Passchendaele line.
November 18th	Handed over to 2nd Canadian Division, and Division moved south.
November 24th	Division arrived in the Auchel-Houdain training area.
December 20th	Took over Acheville-Mericourt-Avion fronts from portions of 1st and 2nd Canadian Divisions.
1918.	
February 20th	Handed over line to 2nd Canadian Division, and moved to Bruay-Auchel area.
March 13th ...	Took over Lens–St. Emile front from 2nd and 1st Canadian Divisions.
March 21st ...	German offensive commenced.
March 24th ...	10th Canadian Infantry Brigade took over Hill 70 front from 1st Canadian Division.
March 29th ...	Division handed over the Lens–St. Emile–Hill 70 fronts to 46th British Division. On this night the Gavrelle-Oppy front was taken over from the 56th British Division.
April 9th ...	German attack on the Lys commenced.
April 12th ...	Division took over Acheville front from 3rd Canadian Division.
April 13th ...	Took over Mericourt front.
May 7th ...	Handed over line to 51st and 52nd Scottish Divisions, and moved back to Monchy Breton area.
May 24th ...	4th Brigade Canadian Engineers officially brought into existence.
July 1st ...	Corps Sports at Tincques.
July 12th ...	Took over Gavrelle-Oppy front.
July 19th ...	Extended frontage as far south as the River Scarpe.
August 2nd ...	Handed over line to 52nd Division, and commenced move to Amiens.

August 8th	Attacked up to " Blue Dotted Line."
August 10th	Capture of Fouquescourt and Chilly.
August 13th	Handed over line to 2nd Canadian Division, and moved to Beaucourt area.
August 17th	Took over line from 2nd Canadian Division.
August 25th	Handed over line to 34th and 35th French Divisions, and moved back towards Amiens.
August 31st — September 1st	12th Canadian Infantry Brigade took over line in front of Queant-Drocourt line.
September 1st/2nd	10th Canadian Infantry Brigade took over line on left of 12th Canadian Infantry Brigade.
September 2nd	Division attacked Queant-Drocourt line.
September 3rd	Division advanced to Canal du Nord.
September 5th	Handed over line to 3rd Canadian Division, and moved back near Arras.
September 26th	Took over front on Canal du Nord opposite Bourlon Wood from 2nd Canadian Division.
September 27th	Captured Bourlon Wood.
September 28th	10th Canadian Infantry Brigade attacked up to Cambrai-Douai Road.
September 29th	12th Canadian Infantry Brigade attacked Sancourt and Blecourt.
September 30th	11th Canadian Infantry Brigade attacked Sancourt and Blecourt and captured railway line.
October 1st	11th Canadian Infantry Brigade continued attack.
October 2nd	Handed over line to 2nd Canadian Division, and moved to Haute Avesnes area.
October 17th	Took over line on Canal de la Sensee from 56th British Division.
October 18th	Crossed canal.
October 20th	Captured Denain.
October 30th	Took over line in front of Mont Houy.
November 1st	10th Canadian Infantry Brigade captured Mont Houy.
November 2nd	Division captured Valenciennes.
November 5th	Re-entered Belgium.
November 6th	Handed over to 2nd Canadian Division, and withdrew to Valenciennes area.
November 11th	Armistice.
November 17th	Moved to Mons.
December 15th	Moved to Jodoigne area.

1919.

January 4th	Moved to Wavre-Waterloo-Boitsfort area.
April 14th	First troops entrained for the Base *en route* for Bramshott Camp.
May 17th	First troops entrained for Southampton *en route* for Canada.
June	Home.

MY FAREWELL

ADIEU ! What volumes this word represents in attempting to bid farewell to you, my comrades and friends ! Words are simply inadequate ; language fails to convey the depth and sincerity of this my message of Godspeed and safe return home.

Never has any Division had more reason for pride in accomplishment of deeds, in heroism, in valour, and in behaviour, life, and conduct. All these attributes make one realize more than ever the loss of that close, intimate association that has bound us together for nearly three years.

Carefully selected from every province in Canada, the units in the 4th Canadian Division are truly representative of our great Dominion, and the comradeship born on so many historic battlefields, nurtured by bitter conditions and hardships, and cemented by ties of common losses of gallant comrades who have made the great sacrifice will, I trust, most indissolubly bind together our future lives in Canada, forming a mysterious yet unbreakable bond between us all, extending from Halifax to Victoria.

And so I take this last opportunity on which we are yet together of thanking you for your loyal, practical work in the Division, and I venture an opinion that we will return to Canada better and greater men, more fitted by that discipline that we have self-imposed, to carry on in Canada that life of acts and deeds calculated in every way in the best interests of our country—a combination of acts and deeds that has been so eminently successful as representative of Canada in the 4th Canadian Division.

And in this parting, when each one of us separates to various centres of our Homeland, let us solemnly and respectfully allow our thoughts and memories to dwell for a few moments with those gallant comrades whom we are leaving behind—men who have made the greatest sacrifice, and whose gallantry and devotion have made it possible that our country and our posterity shall live in freedom and security for all time to come.

May I state in conclusion my hope that, in years to come, if my services can be of any assistance to any of my comrades in the Division, there shall be no hesitation in calling on me, as I shall be only too glad to do anything in my power at any time.

S. Watson

MAJOR-GENERAL.

www.ingramcontent.com/pod-product-compliance
Lightning Source LLC
Chambersburg PA
CBHW060222050426
42446CB00013B/3139